Etiquette
The least you need to know

JAMILA MUSAYEVA

Jamila Musayeva. *Etiquette, The Least You Need to Know*

All rights reserved. No part of this publication may be copied, reproduced, stored in a retrieval system, or transmitted in any form or by any means, electronic or mechanical (including photocopying, electronic, recording, or otherwise) without the prior permission in writing from the publisher and copyright owner.

Illustrations by: Rauf Valiyev

Book Design: www.adamhaystudio.com

ISBN: 978-0-578-44770-4

© Jamila Musayeva, 2019
© TEAS Press Publishing House. Baku, 2019

www.teaspress.az

Notice of Liability
This publication contains the opinions and ideas of its author. It is intended to provide informative, inspirational, and helpful material on the subjects addressed in the publication. The author specifically disclaims all responsibility for any liability, loss or risk, personal or otherwise, which is caused directly or indirectly by the use and application of any of the contents of this publication.

Printed in Turkey

Dedicated to my family

About the Author

Jamila Musayeva is a certified international social etiquette consultant and co-founder of Gymbala – the first gym for toddlers and children in Azerbaijan. A summa cum laude graduate of the George Washington University in Washington, D.C., with a degree in international relations, she is passionate about foreign languages, cultures, and education. Jamila holds a Master in European Political and Governance Studies, and is a member of the Golden Key International Honour Society and Phi Beta Kappa. She currently resides in Baku, Azerbaijan, with her husband and two beautiful children, Sevinj and Jamil.

CONTENTS

	So, what exactly is etiquette?	8
	The five basic principles	12
I.	**Traveling to**	14
	Walking the stairs: ladies first, or not?	16
	Walking on the road: choose your side	20
	In and out of the Elevator	24
II.	**Arriving**	30
	How late is too late?	32
	To gift or not to gift: any gift is better than no gift	36
	Decode dress codes	42
III.	**All about table manners**	56
	Where shall I sit?	58
	The napkin affair	62
	What is what? Let the cutlery speak for itself	70
	The "B" plate	74
	Know your glass	78
	Your four-course table setup	92
	Hold your cutlery	96
	Cutlery language: take it or leave it	100
	Eat your soup	102
	Serving: where to expect the food	106
	Salt and pepper go together	110
	Finger bowl	112
	Have your dessert and eat it, too	114
	Leaving the dinner table	116
IV.	**Leaving: saying your "goodbye" and "thank you"**	118
V.	**The Don'ts of table manners**	122
	A Final Word	146

ETIQUETTE
THE LEAST YOU NEED TO KNOW

So, what exactly is etiquette?

According to the Oxford Dictionary, *etiquette* means "the customary code of behaviour in a society or among members of a particular profession or group."

The term originated from the Old French word *estiquette*, which means "a label" or "a ticket." Back in the seventeenth century, a fancy French king named Louis XIV had a beautiful palace in Versailles with well-groomed gardens. His gardener took meticulous care of the gardens and put a label – étiquet – on the grass to warn the noblemen to stay off. (That's right, even aristocrats were not well-mannered then.) What was initially a warning sign on the grass ultimately evolved into a set of "do's" and "don'ts": prior to attending an event at the palace, guests were given a "ticket" outlining the rules of proper behaviour.

ETIQUETTE
THE LEAST YOU NEED TO KNOW

Over time, etiquette evolved both in its meaning and importance. Up until the 1960s, after completing formal education, young women were expected to attend one year of finishing school before stepping into society. As the term "finishing" implies, these schools were meant to add finishing touches to a student's education. Women were taught the essentials of etiquette and good manners. One of the prominent finishing schools that still functions today is Institut Villa Pierrefeu, founded in 1954 in Montreux, Switzerland, by Dorette Faillettaz.

The word "etiquette" is often used interchangeably with the word "manners." Either way, mastering etiquette rules and having good manners goes a long, long, long way! As U.S. Supreme Court Justice Clarence Thomas once said, "Good manners will open doors that the best education cannot." A Yale University graduate, Mr. Thomas definitely knew what he was talking about. After all, it is not the diploma that others see first, but manners and looks.

Let's get started - it is never too soon or too late to learn good manners.

ETIQUETTE
THE LEAST YOU NEED TO KNOW

The five basic principles

Everything about etiquette is logical, intuitive, and functional.

ETIQUETTE
THE LEAST YOU NEED TO KNOW

Here are five basic principles to remember:

1.
Do not stand out. Make as little movement and noise as you can. The less you are noticed, the better mannered you are deemed.

2.
When it comes to cutlery and glassware, form takes after function. The shape of an item of cutlery or a glass carries a specific purpose. If you are uncertain about the purpose of a particular item on the table, pay attention to its design and let it speak for itself.

3.
When in doubt, observe. Watch others and follow their lead. If a majority does something, even if it is wrongly done, follow the group and you will not stand out. Do not be the only one in the room eating a banana with a fork and knife (albeit correctly, according to etiquette) if everyone else is using their hands. Do not be the odd one out.

4.
Manners are noticed first – so let them work in your favor.

5.
Master the rules of etiquette. Prepare and practice them at home until good manners are your second nature and you no longer have to think twice about them.

ETIQUETTE
THE LEAST YOU NEED TO KNOW

Traveling to

ETIQUETTE
THE LEAST YOU NEED TO KNOW

Walking the stairs: ladies first, or not?

When going upstairs, ladies go first.

ETIQUETTE
THE LEAST YOU NEED TO KNOW

If you are a host, you should always precede your guest on the stairs. In all cases, ascend on the right side and descend on the left.

ETIQUETTE
WALKING THE STAIRS

When descending, the man goes before the lady to make sure he can catch her in case she slips and falls. It's not the most desirable scenario, but if it does happen, he should always be there for her to fall back on – literally.

ETIQUETTE
THE LEAST YOU NEED TO KNOW

Walking on the road: choose your side

Which side of the road do you think is more dangerous to walk on: closer to the cars or away from them? You guessed it right – closer to the cars, of course.

ETIQUETTE
THE LEAST YOU NEED TO KNOW

Hence, men are expected to walk on the more dangerous side of the road, thereby protecting ladies from traffic.

ETIQUETTE
WALKING ON THE ROAD

If you are a parent walking with a child, you should walk closer to the traffic regardless of your gender.

ETIQUETTE
THE LEAST YOU NEED TO KNOW

In and out of the elevator

When entering or exiting an elevator, ladies always go first, with the door held by men.

ETIQUETTE
IN AND OUT OF THE ELEVATOR

ETIQUETTE
THE LEAST YOU NEED TO KNOW

If you are going to the top floor, make sure you stand at the very back of the elevator so you will not have to get in and out every time the elevator stops at the floors beneath yours.

ETIQUETTE
IN AND OUT OF THE ELEVATOR

ETIQUETTE
THE LEAST YOU NEED TO KNOW

If the elevator is packed, those closest to the elevator door get in and out first. Even if they have not arrived at their floor, they should step out, allow those from the back of the elevator to get out, and then get back in.

ETIQUETTE
IN AND OUT OF THE ELEVATOR

II

ETIQUETTE
THE LEAST YOU NEED TO KNOW

Arriving

ETIQUETTE
THE LEAST YOU NEED TO KNOW

How late is too late?

Invited by a German, arrive like a German.
When you are invited to someone's home for a dinner or any other occasion, please make sure to arrive on time. Arriving early is a big no-no. If you arrive even five minutes earlier than expected, you might find yourself in an awkward situation: either the dinner table is not fully set, or your host is running around in their homewear.

ETIQUETTE
HOW LATE IS TOO LATE?

ETIQUETTE
THE LEAST YOU NEED TO KNOW

Arriving late is a bit trickier.
How late is too late and the degree of acceptable lateness varies from culture to culture. For example, if you are invited to a German person's home, arrive like a German – meaning, be strictly on time. Germans have a reputation for punctuality, and as a guest at a German house, you should be punctual too. Make sure you know the degree of lateness that is acceptable to your host and allow yourself to be late accordingly.

ETIQUETTE
HOW LATE IS TOO LATE?

ETIQUETTE
THE LEAST YOU NEED TO KNOW

To gift or not to gift: any gift is better than no gift

ETIQUETTE
TO GIFT OR NOT TO GIFT

ETIQUETTE
THE LEAST YOU NEED TO KNOW

When you are invited to someone's home or dinner party, make sure you bring them a little gift. Remember that any gift is better than no gift. If you are wondering what such a gift might be, here are some ideas:

A box of chocolates
A scented candle
A good book

ETIQUETTE
TO GIFT OR NOT TO GIFT

ETIQUETTE
THE LEAST YOU NEED TO KNOW

Flowers in a vase.
Why a vase? Because you will save your host the hassle of finding an appropriate vase for the flowers you just brought. What if your host does not even own one? Take that extra step and guarantee yourself a second invitation. A well-prepared and well-mannered guest is always a pleasure to host.

ETIQUETTE
TO GIFT OR NOT TO GIFT

ETIQUETTE
THE LEAST YOU NEED TO KNOW

Decode dress codes

ETIQUETTE
DECODE DRESS CODES

RECEPTION

please join us for
DINNER, DRINKS AND DANCING
20:00
Plaza Hotel
768 5th Ave
New York, NY

Cocktail Attire

ETIQUETTE
THE LEAST YOU NEED TO KNOW

White Tie

Very rarely you will be requested to dress in the most formal of all dress codes: "white tie." If you are asked, though, you have probably been invited to a royal wedding, a formal ball, or a gala evening. Under this dress code, men wear black tailcoat jackets, high-waisted tuxedo trousers, a white tuxedo shirt, a white waistcoat, a white bow tie, and black leather shoes. White gloves and a top hat are also permissible, though not mandatory. Women wear full-length evening gowns with covered shoulders and their hair in an updo. This is the time for women to bring out their most dazzling jewelry items – tiaras, for example, are welcomed.

ETIQUETTE
DECODE DRESS CODES

ETIQUETTE
THE LEAST YOU NEED TO KNOW

Black Tie

Black tie is the most frequently requested dress code at formal occasions, such as weddings and fancy dinner parties. At a black tie event, women are expected to wear a floor-length gown with open or covered shoulders and any hairstyle they wish. Jewelry or bijouterie is welcomed (leave your tiara at home, though). Men wear a dinner jacket, a white dress shirt, a black bow tie, a waistcoat or cummerbund, and black shoes.

ETIQUETTE
DECODE DRESS CODES

ETIQUETTE
THE LEAST YOU NEED TO KNOW

Cocktail Attire

A cocktail attire dress code is usually applicable for any outing, dinner date, or birthday party. Ladies can wear any length of party dress they like (a little black dress is always a good idea!). Alternatively, a nice fancy skirt and a blouse is also suitable. Gents wear a dark-colored suit (charcoal grey, navy, dark brown – get creative) with or without a tie.

ETIQUETTE
DECODE DRESS CODES

ETIQUETTE
THE LEAST YOU NEED TO KNOW

Business Formal

You might be asked to wear business formal attire for a job interview, a networking event, a presentation, or a meeting with a big client. Ladies can wear dress pants or a dress skirt with a jacket and a blouse or shirt. Men should wear a suit, a button-up shirt with a collar, and a tie. The darker the outfit, the more formal the look.

ETIQUETTE
DECODE DRESS CODES

ETIQUETTE
THE LEAST YOU NEED TO KNOW

Smart/Business Casual

As its name implies, business casual is in between business formal and casual. You should not look like you are about to meet an important client and certainly not like you are going to the movies. Men can wear a t-shirt of any color, a blazer or a sweater, and jeans or pants. Women have a wide range of clothing to choose from both in terms of color and length: a casual dress, skirt, jeans or pants, a blouse or a shirt, a blazer, or a sweater.

ETIQUETTE
DECODE DRESS CODES

ETIQUETTE
THE LEAST YOU NEED TO KNOW

Casual Wear

A casual dress code is all about comfort. If you are invited to someone's home and there is no specific dress code required, assume that casual wear is acceptable. Casual wear is anything you wear in your everyday life. There are no rules here. Wear whatever feels comfortable – jeans, a hoodie, shorts, a dress, and so on.

ETIQUETTE
DECODE DRESS CODES

ETIQUETTE
THE LEAST YOU NEED TO KNOW

All about table manners

ETIQUETTE
THE LEAST YOU NEED TO KNOW

Where shall I sit?

If there are name cards on a dinner table, just find your name and sit at your assigned seat.

ETIQUETTE
WHERE SHALL I SIT

ETIQUETTE
THE LEAST YOU NEED TO KNOW

However, if there are no name cards, wait for your host to guide you to your place. If you are at a small dinner party, wait for the host to take his or her seat first before taking yours. Usually the hosts (H and H2) sit at the short ends of the table, opposite each other. The most honorable guest (G) sits at the host's right-hand side (this is for convenience, because the host will serve the food to the guest from the right).

If you are a man, help the lady on your right to be seated before taking your seat. The best seats are considered the ones with the best view, so save a seat with a view for the person you are honoring that night – be it your date or a guest of honor.

ETIQUETTE
WHERE SHALL I SIT

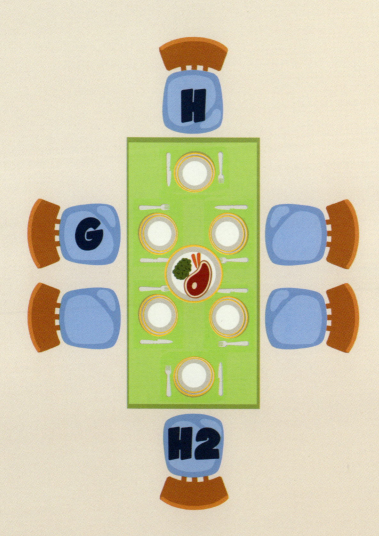

ETIQUETTE
THE LEAST YOU NEED TO KNOW

The napkin affair

A napkin is like the child of a tablecloth and a tissue. In terms of its design, just like a tablecloth, a napkin is also made of cloth – but it is much smaller. In terms of its functionality, it is meant to keep your mouth, hands, and lap clean but not in the way that a tissue does.

ETIQUETTE
THE NAPKIN AFFAIR

ETIQUETTE
THE LEAST YOU NEED TO KNOW

Remember, you should *never* wipe your face with a napkin. What you *can* do is gently dab your lips and fingers with a napkin to clean them, and when not using it, keep it on your lap to protect your clothing.

ETIQUETTE
THE NAPKIN AFFAIR

ETIQUETTE
THE LEAST YOU NEED TO KNOW

If you have a large napkin, fold it in half before placing it on your lap.

If you are given a small napkin, unfold it completely before placing it on your lap.

Do not cover your neck with it, fold it back into its original shape, or put it on your plate. If you accidentally drop it, you can pick it up and continue using it (if that's okay with you) or ask your waiter for a clean one.

ETIQUETTE
THE NAPKIN AFFAIR

ETIQUETTE
THE LEAST YOU NEED TO KNOW

Let's learn the "napkin language."
Your napkin will communicate different
messages to a waiter depending
on its placement.

Here, the position of your napkin says,
"I am coming back to the table. Save my spot."

Once done using it, simply fold it neatly
and put it to the left of your plate. Placed
this way, it means "I am not coming back
to the table."

ETIQUETTE
THE NAPKIN AFFAIR

ETIQUETTE
THE LEAST YOU NEED TO KNOW

What is what? Let the cutlery speak for itself

Remember how you learned earlier that the form of a cutlery takes after its function? The larger the meal, the bigger the cutlery. If the knife has a sharp blade, expect to be served steak. If you are served a meal with a blunt-bladed knife, then you are probably not supposed to use the knife to cut, but rather to tear apart or separate your food. If you are served a creamy soup, the spoon will be more round and wide to accommodate the creamy texture. Since broth soup is light and watery, you will be given a standard oval-shaped spoon to eat it with. The serving spoon and serving fork are there for you to serve yourself the meal, not to eat with (they are way too large).

ETIQUETTE
THE LEAST YOU NEED TO KNOW

Here are the most frequently used items of cutlery. There are some unusual ones not included, like the oyster fork. If you want to see these, Google "seafood cutlery items."

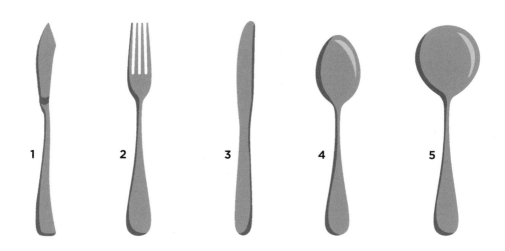

1. Butter knife
2. Main course fork
3. Main course knife
4. Broth soup spoon
5. Cream soup spoon

ETIQUETTE
LET CUTLERY SPEAK FOR ITSELF

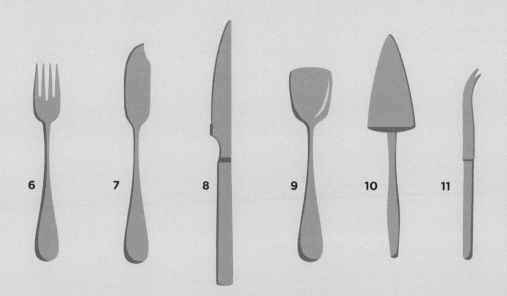

6. Fish fork
7. Fish knife
8. Steak knife
9. Ice cream spoon
10. Cake server
11. Cheese knife

ETIQUETTE
THE LEAST YOU NEED TO KNOW

The "B" plate

Connect your left thumb with your left index finger. See how you have formed the letter "b"? Use this as a reminder that your bread plate and butter knife are placed together on the upper left side of your dinner plate.

ETIQUETTE
THE "B" PLATE

ETIQUETTE
THE LEAST YOU NEED TO KNOW

The butter knife is usually placed on the bread plate. It is much smaller than your main dinner knife. Also, unlike other knives, the butter knife has dull blades since it is used for spreading the butter, not for cutting it.

If you cannot remember which cutlery is for what purpose, just remember that form takes after function. Look at a knife, imagine what you can use it for, and then see if you are right.

ETIQUETTE
THE "B" PLATE

ETIQUETTE
THE LEAST YOU NEED TO KNOW

Know your glass

Now, connect your right thumb with your right index finger. Do you see how you have formed a letter "d"? "D" stands for "drinks." Your drink glasses are usually placed at the upper right corner above your dinner plate (because the majority of us are right-handed and we pick up our glasses using our right hand). The glasses are placed in height order.

Why? So you can easily pick up the tall glasses without knocking down the shorter ones. Imagine if the glasses were placed the other way around. Would it be comfortable to pick up a small glass if it was "hidden" behind a tall one? Remember that everything in etiquette is logical, intuitive, and functional.

ETIQUETTE
KNOW YOUR GLASS

ETIQUETTE
THE LEAST YOU NEED TO KNOW

Another tip to help you remember the glass arrangement: think of it like a family Christmas photo. The tall family members always stand behind the shorter ones, who occupy the first row.

ETIQUETTE
KNOW YOUR GLASS

ETIQUETTE
THE LEAST YOU NEED TO KNOW

Red wine glass

Hold by the bottom of the bowl.

ETIQUETTE
KNOW YOUR GLASS

ETIQUETTE
THE LEAST YOU NEED TO KNOW

Space for unusual drinks
(like a VIP drink)

Champagne glasses are long and thin. Hold this type of glass by the stem to avoid warming up your drink.

ÈTIQUETTE
KNOW YOUR GLASS

ETIQUETTE
THE LEAST YOU NEED TO KNOW

Water glass

Usually has no stem, therefore you hold it firmly by its lower part. However, water can also be served in a goblet, which is taller than a wine glass. In this case, it is placed at the back.

ETIQUETTE
KNOW YOUR GLASS

ETIQUETTE
THE LEAST YOU NEED TO KNOW

White wine glass

Smaller and shorter than a red wine glass.
Hold by the stem so as not to warm it up.

Why should you hold certain glasses by the stem?
In order to avoid warming the drink up with your hand.
No one likes to drink warm champagne or wine.

ETIQUETTE
KNOW YOUR GLASS

ETIQUETTE
THE LEAST YOU NEED TO KNOW

"No more, please"

If a waiter is pouring you a drink and you do not want it, either leave it (if you did not see the waiter pouring it) or gently touch your glass (hinting "no more, please"). Do *not* cover the glass with your hands!

ETIQUETTE
KNOW YOUR GLASS

ETIQUETTE
THE LEAST YOU NEED TO KNOW

Your four-course table setup

What do you think is on our menu today? Looking at the image, this is what our menu looks like in the order of serving:

Soup
Salad
Main course
Dessert

ETIQUETTE
YOUR FOUR-COURSE TABLE SETUP

ETIQUETTE
THE LEAST YOU NEED TO KNOW

When it comes to cutlery, remember that we always start from the outside right. The cutlery that is placed first from the outside will be used first – this is practical and logical. As the meals are served and cleared, the cutlery from the further end will be cleared and the ones closer to our dish will remain. Also, bear in mind that the cutlery is usually placed in pairs on left and right sides of the plate. If there is a piece of cutlery that is not part of a pair, use it alone. For example, the soup spoon is the odd one on the right, so it will be used alone to eat the soup. Following is the pairing of fish fork (left of the plate) and fish knife (right of the plate) – use them both to eat the fish.

The golden rule is that there should be no more than three pieces of cutlery on each side of the plate (but there are exceptions when the menu is larger). The dessert cutlery (spoon and fork) is usually placed above the plate. Why? Because remember – there are no more than three pieces on each side, and also you do not need dessert cutlery until the very end of the meal. Once your other cutlery is cleared away after the main course, the dessert cutlery is simply placed to the sides of your dish: fork on the left and spoon on the right. You may now eat your dessert.

ETIQUETTE
YOUR FOUR-COURSE TABLE SETUP

ETIQUETTE
THE LEAST YOU NEED TO KNOW

Hold your cutlery

There are two main styles with which to hold cutlery: the Continental style (also known as the European style) and the American style. Eating in the American style, you cut the food one piece at a time and keep switching your fork from your left hand to your right hand.

ETIQUETTE
HOLD YOUR CUTLERY

Using the American style, you can hold your fork this way.

ETIQUETTE
THE LEAST YOU NEED TO KNOW

Do *not* put used cutlery back on the table.
Once it touches your meal, it stays on the dish.

Another good rule to remember: if you are given a "solitary" cutlery, such as a fork, then place it in your right hand. If you are given a fork paired with a spoon or a knife, then place the fork in your left hand. Spoons and knives are always placed in your right hand.

ETIQUETTE
HOLD YOUR CUTLERY

Using the Continental style, you keep your fork in your left hand and your knife in your right hand for the entire duration of your meal, like this:

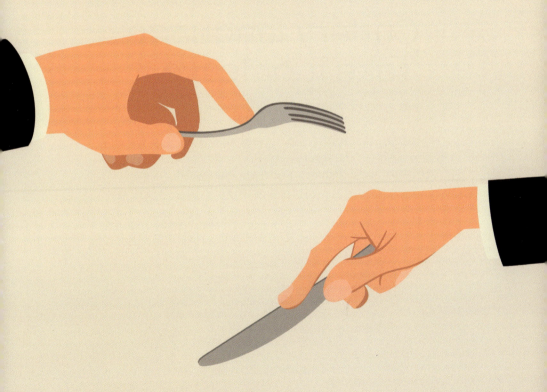

ETIQUETTE
THE LEAST YOU NEED TO KNOW

Cutlery language: take it or leave it

There is no need to wave at the waiter to come pick up your dish. Simply use your cutlery to communicate. If you are done with your meal, position your cutlery accordingly – the waiter will know what to do. The less attention you draw to yourself, the better mannered you will appear.

Always remember: the blades of the knives should always face inward. If you only use a fork, then leave it with prongs facing up.

ETIQUETTE
CUTLERY LANGUAGE

Resting Position
Acceptable positions

Done Position
Acceptable positions

10 o'clock and 4 o'clock   12 o'clock and 6 o'clock

ETIQUETTE
THE LEAST YOU NEED TO KNOW

Eat your soup

Most of us do not eat our soup the right way. What is the correct way to do it? First, pick up the spoon and dip it into the soup at the center of the bowl. Next, move the spoon towards the opposite end of the bowl and gently tap the spoon on the edge, and then bring the spoon to your mouth.

ETIQUETTE
EAT YOUR SOUP

ETIQUETTE
THE LEAST YOU NEED TO KNOW

Eating your soup this way might seem a bit odd at first, but bear in mind that the rules of etiquette have a practical and logical purpose. The purpose of scooping the soup away from ourselves is to make sure that the soup-filled spoon leaves its dripping bits on the opposite end of the bowl (where we gently tap the bottom of the spoon to clear it off) and only after makes its way to our mouth. You can either drink the soup from the end or the side of the spoon.

If you are served a soup in a bowl with two handles, then feel free to drink your soup directly from the bowl. Please, never blow on your soup.

ETIQUETTE
THE LEAST YOU NEED TO KNOW

Serving: where to expect the food

If a waiter is serving the food, expect him or her to arrive from your left to deliver the food, and to pick it up from your right.

This rule has its purpose: to avoid spillage of food. While you are actively using your cutlery to cut food, the chances of you bumping into the waiter from your right are higher than from your left side. Hence, the waiter arrives from the left to serve you the food.

ETIQUETTE
SERVING: WHERE TO EXPECT IT

ETIQUETTE
THE LEAST YOU NEED TO KNOW

If there is no waiter, then feel free to ask someone to pass you the food if it is placed far away from you. Please do not stand and reach for it. If you are in charge of passing the food, always pass it to your right and expect it to arrive back to you from the left side.

ETIQUETTE
SERVING: WHERE TO EXPECT IT

ETIQUETTE
THE LEAST YOU NEED TO KNOW

Salt and pepper go together

If you are asked to pass the salt, do not forget to pass it together with the pepper. These two belong together no matter what is asked for.

Just for your reference, salt shakers in Europe have tinier and more holes than pepper shakers. In the United States, it is the opposite.

ETIQUETTE
SALT AND PEPPER GO TOGETHER

ETIQUETTE
THE LEAST YOU NEED TO KNOW

Finger bowl

Prior to dessert at a formal dinner party, you may be served a "finger bowl" – a bowl of warm water, sometimes with slices of lemon or flower petals for a fragrant touch. Think of it as a fancy version of wet wipes.

Simply immerse the tips of your fingers into the water, one hand at a time, and then gently pat your fingers dry on the napkin that is placed on your lap. You can also brush your wet fingers on your mouth and then dab your mouth with a napkin. The purpose of a finger bowl is to save you the hassle of leaving the table and going to the loo to wash your hands.

ETIQUETTE
FINGER BOWL

ETIQUETTE
THE LEAST YOU NEED TO KNOW

Have your dessert and eat it, too

Depending on what you are served for dessert, you might be given a fork and a spoon or a spoon alone. If you are served a fork and a spoon together, the fork functions as the "holder" of the dessert while the spoon acts as a knife to cut it. Once a piece of dessert is cut, the spoon goes back to fulfilling its original function – to carry the dessert to your mouth –while the fork switches its role to help push the dessert crumbles to your spoon.

It sounds complicated, but simply put: if the dessert is served with a fork and a spoon, hold and push with the fork and cut and eat with the spoon. If you are only served one item of cutlery, then use it for all purposes. For example, pie or cake is often served with a fork only, and ice cream is served with a spoon only; but ice cream together with cake is served with both a fork and a spoon.

ETIQUETTE
HAVE YOUR DESSERT AND EAT IT, TOO

ETIQUETTE
THE LEAST YOU NEED TO KNOW

Leaving the dinner table

If you are at a large table and you need to use the loo, excuse yourself to those nearest to you and leave the table. You do not need to announce your departure to everyone at the table. At formal dinner parties, you should not leave the table until dessert is served. This means you should visit the loo prior to joining the dinner table and hold any "emergencies" until dessert time.

The general rule is not to leave the table until your host stands up and leaves his or her napkin on the table (a sign indicating "time to leave the table"). Younger people should not leave the table before elders. In this day and age, some of these etiquette rules are broken, but it is good to know them just in case you happen to be invited to a formal dinner party.

ETIQUETTE
LEAVING THE DINNER TABLE

IV

ETIQUETTE
THE LEAST YOU NEED TO KNOW

Leaving:
saying your goodbye and thank you

ETIQUETTE
THE LEAST YOU NEED TO KNOW

Just like when you arrive, be sure to leave the party on time. "On time" means do not leave too early and do not overstay. Look for clues as to when it is time to leave – perhaps other guests have left already, or your host is yawning or checking the time. Bear in mind that hosting a dinner party can be very tiring, so do not exhaust your host. Do not stay for so long that your host hopes you leave. Leave on time so he or she hopes you come back.

If you happen to have to leave the party early, see the host and excuse yourself for your early departure. Do not leave without saying goodbye to the host unless it is an emergency or the party is so big that the host is busy entertaining other people. In those rare cases, you can "ghost," or leave without saying goodbye.

While it is sometimes acceptable to leave without saying goodbye, it is never acceptable not to thank your host. Do not be stingy with your compliments. Thank your host as many times as you can – it will never hurt. A brief message or phone call to say "thank you" the day after the party is a must. If you want to take an extra step to show your gratitude, write a handwritten "thank you" note. You will be remembered for this gesture.

A good guest is someone who is punctual, well-mannered, considerate, and thankful. Be a good guest.

ETIQUETTE
LEAVING: SAYING YOUR GOODBYE AND THANK YOU

V

ETIQUETTE
THE LEAST YOU NEED TO KNOW

The Don'ts of table manners

ETIQUETTE
THE LEAST YOU NEED TO KNOW

Your personal belongings do not belong on the table unless they are edible (phones and handbags are no exception).

ETIQUETTE
THE DON'TS OF TABLE MANNERS

No texting at a formal dinner party.
Leave your phone in your handbag or pocket.

ETIQUETTE
THE LEAST YOU NEED TO KNOW

If you do not want a refill for your drink, politely say so.
Do not flip over your glass.

ETIQUETTE
THE DON'TS OF TABLE MANNERS

If you want to use a toothpick, excuse yourself from the table and do so in the loo – never at the table. Even if you cover your mouth with your hands, we still see what you are doing there …

ETIQUETTE
THE LEAST YOU NEED TO KNOW

Do not place your elbows on the table.
It is plain rude.

ETIQUETTE
THE DON'TS OF TABLE MANNERS

Always close your mouth when you are chewing food. Nobody wants to see the process.

ETIQUETTE
THE LEAST YOU NEED TO KNOW

If you are at a big table and want a dish that is placed far from you, do not stand up and lean over to reach for it. First, you look funny doing that, and second, you will surely stain your clothing. Simply ask someone closer to the dish to pass it to you.

ETIQUETTE
THE DON'TS OF TABLE MANNERS

Never drink anything with your pinkie sticking out.
It is simply bad manners.

ETIQUETTE
THE LEAST YOU NEED TO KNOW

Adding milk first and then tea.

ETIQUETTE
THE DON'TS OF TABLE MANNERS

Always serve your tea first and then add milk.

ETIQUETTE
THE LEAST YOU NEED TO KNOW

You are not Winnie-the-Pooh.
Napkins belong on your lap, not on your neck.

ETIQUETTE
THE DON'TS OF TABLE MANNERS

Never use a knife to cut bread. The small knife on your bread plate, known as a butter knife, is for spreading butter - not for cutting bread.

ETIQUETTE
THE LEAST YOU NEED TO KNOW

Holding your cutlery while having a conversation makes you look quite hostile. Leave your fork and knife at a resting position while having a conversation.

ETIQUETTE
THE DON'TS OF TABLE MANNERS

The end of a spoon can poke you in the eye if left in a cup when you drink from it, so for safety reasons it is better to take your spoon out of your cup as soon as you have finished stirring your tea or coffee.

ETIQUETTE
THE LEAST YOU NEED TO KNOW

While it is acceptable to eat a chicken thigh with your hands at home, it is better to stick to using a fork and knife when at a formal dinner party.

ETIQUETTE
THE DON'TS OF TABLE MANNERS

Do not ever push away your dirty plate at a dinner party.
Leave your plate where it is. The waiter will pick it up.

ETIQUETTE
THE LEAST YOU NEED TO KNOW

Please refrain from spitting out your food at the table, regardless of its taste. If you really want to spit out the food for whatever reason, excuse yourself and attend the loo.

ETIQUETTE
THE DON'TS OF TABLE MANNERS

If you want to take a break and sip some water in between meals, by all means do so, but leave your cutlery at a resting position before taking your glass.

ETIQUETTE
THE LEAST YOU NEED TO KNOW

If you happen to drop an item of cutlery on the floor, do not pick it up. Just ask for a new one.

ETIQUETTE
THE DON'TS OF TABLE MANNERS

If you are at a table of four to six people, wait for others to join before you commence your meal. Dinners are to be enjoyed together, not solo.

ETIQUETTE
THE LEAST YOU NEED TO KNOW

Never groom yourself at a dinner table.
The "ladies' room" is meant exactly for that use.

ETIQUETTE
THE DON'TS OF TABLE MANNERS

If you do not want a drink refill, just say so.
Do not ever cover a glass with your hands.

A Final Word
I hope you enjoyed reading this book as much as I have enjoyed writing it. I also hope that the knowledge you have gained from reading this book will open new doors for you, previously unimagined. If this book was useful to you in any way, I will be more than happy to hear about it.

Please share your stories with me at
jamila.gasimova@coleurope.eu